Our Bodies

Our Brains

Charlotte Guillain

Heinemann Library
Chicago, Illinois

www.heinemannraintree.com
Visit our website to find out
more information about
Heinemann-Raintree books.

To order:

☎ Phone 888-454-2279
⌨ Visit www.heinemannraintree.com
  to browse our catalog and order online.

Editorial: Rebecca Rissman, Laura Knowles, Nancy Dickmann,
 and Sian Smith
Picture research: Ruth Blair and Mica Brancic
Designed by Joanna Hinton-Malivoire
Original Illustrations © Capstone Global Library Ltd. 2010
Illustrated by Tony Wilson
Printed and bound by Leo Paper Group

14 13 12 11 10
10 9 8 7 6 5 4 3 2 1

Library of Congress Cataloging-in-Publication Data
Guillain, Charlotte.
  Our brains / Charlotte Guillain.
    p. cm. -- (Our bodies)
  Includes bibliographical references and index.
  ISBN 978-1-4329-3592-4 (hc) -- ISBN 978-1-4329-3601-3 (pb)
1. Brain--Juvenile literature. I. Title.
  QP361.5.G85 2010
  612.8'2--dc22
                          2009022296

Acknowledgments
The author and publisher are grateful to the following for
permission to reproduce copyright material:
Corbis pp.**4** (© Tim Pannell), **10** (© Solus-Veer), **14** (© LWA-Dann
Tardif/zefa), **17** (© Roy Morsch/zefa), **20** (© Fancy/Veer), **22** (© Tim
Pannell); iStockphoto pp.**12**, **19** (© Mark Kalkwarf), **21** (© Julián
Rovagnati), **23** (© Mark Kalkwarf); Photolibrary pp.**5** (© Goodshoot),
8 (© Glow Images), **9** (© White), **13** (© Glow Images), **15** (© Banana
Stock), **16** (© Corbis), **18**, **23** (© Asia Images); Science Photo Library
p.**11** (© Geoff Tompkinson).

Front cover photograph of children doing a jigsaw puzzle reproduced
with permission of Corbis (© Randy Faris). Back cover photograph
reproduced with permission of Photolibrary (© Corbis).

Every effort has been made to contact copyright holders of any
material reproduced in this book. Any omissions will be rectified in
subsequent printings if notice is given to the publisher.

Contents

Body Parts

Our bodies have many parts.

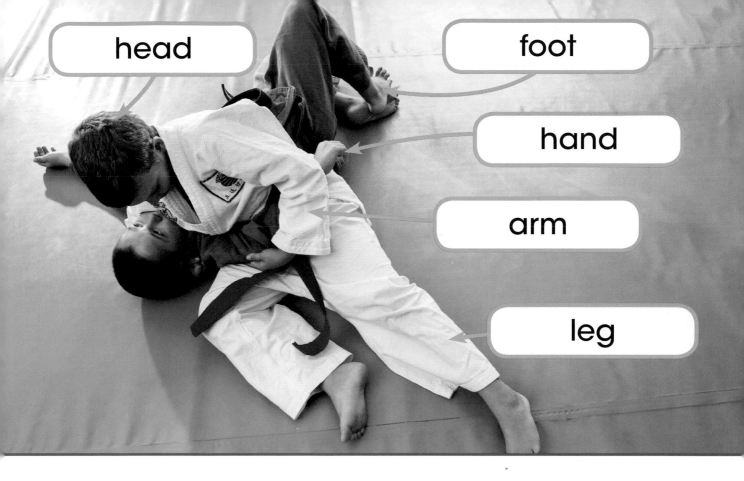

head

foot

hand

arm

leg

Our bodies have parts on the outside.

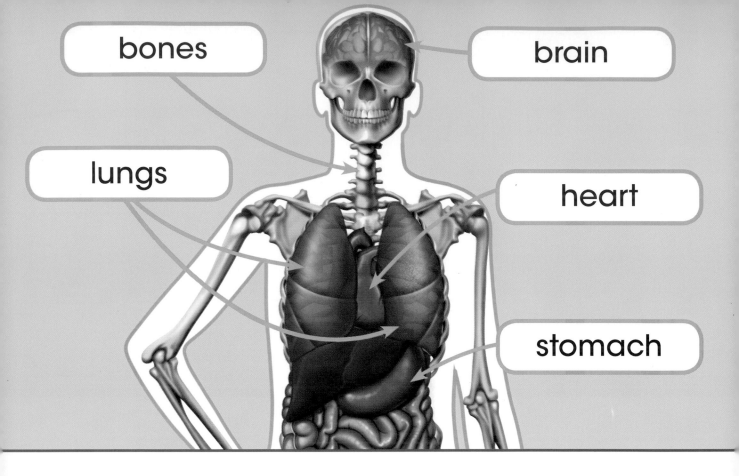

bones

brain

lungs

heart

stomach

Our bodies have parts on
the inside.

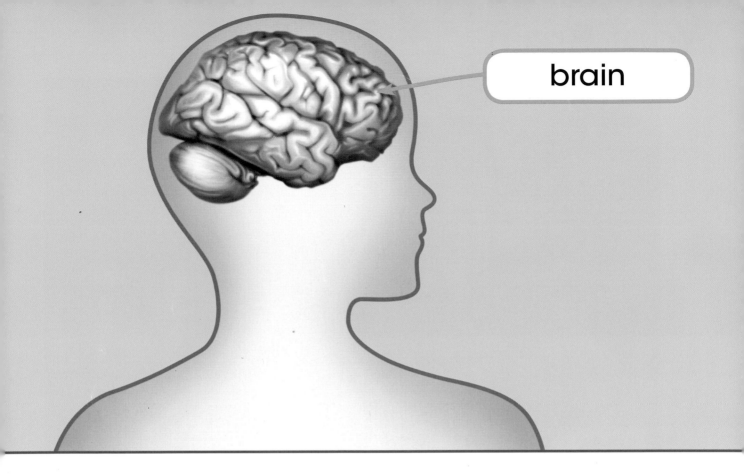

brain

Your brain is inside your body.

Your Brain

You cannot see your brain.

head

Your brain is inside your head.

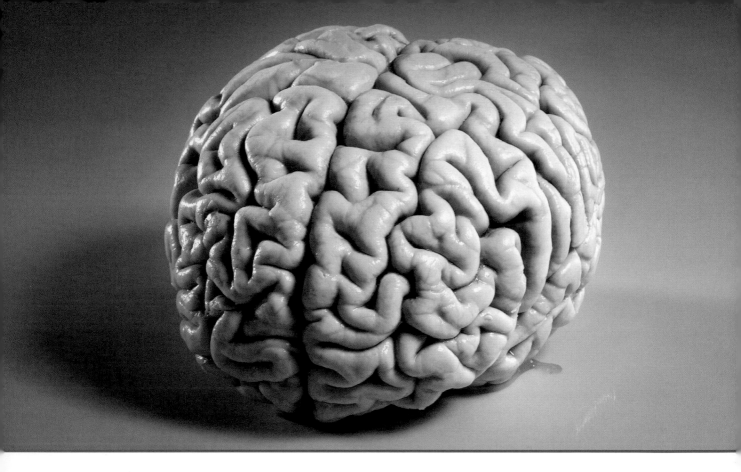

Your brain is wrinkly.

Your brain is soft.

Your Working Brain

Your brain tells your body what to do.

Your brain tells your body how to
do things.

Your brain works when you
are thinking.

Your brain works when you
are moving.

Your brain works when you
are listening.

Your brain works all the time.

Staying Healthy

You can get a lot of rest to help your brain.

You can do puzzles to help
your brain.

You can eat healthy food to help your brain.

You can drink a lot of water to help your brain.

Quiz

Where in your body is your brain?

22

Answer on page 24

Picture Glossary

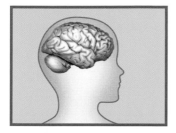

brain part of your body inside your head. You think with your brain. Your brain tells your body what to do.

puzzle game that gives you a problem to work out

rest to take time to relax and not do very much

Index

Answer to quiz on page 22: Your brain is in your head.

Notes to parents and teachers
Before reading
Ask children to name the parts of their body they can see on the outside. Then ask them what parts of their body are inside. Make a list of them together and see if the children know what each body part does, for example, stomachs break down food. Discuss where their brain is and ask if anyone knows what brains do.

After reading
Play a memory game. Put the children into groups and give each group a tray, a cloth, and ten small objects. Demonstrate the game by showing them ten objects on a tray and then covering the tray with a cloth. Remove one object without letting the children see, and then remove the cloth and ask them which object is missing. Then ask them to play the game in their groups, taking turns hiding objects and guessing.